Original title:
Tides of Peace

Copyright © 2025 Creative Arts Management OÜ
All rights reserved.

Author: Colin Leclair
ISBN HARDBACK: 978-1-80581-608-9
ISBN PAPERBACK: 978-1-80581-135-0
ISBN EBOOK: 978-1-80581-608-9

Reflections of a Gentle Mind

In a world of flocks and fowls,
The cat counts sheep, it purrs and growls.
A zenful squirrel with a nut to chew,
Wonders how deep the rabbit hole flew.

Seagulls squawk in a comical dance,
Chasing sandwiches, they take a chance.
A wise old tortoise, slow and grand,
Knows each shell has a secret plan.

Oasis of Calm in the Chaos

A lemonade stand in the stormy rain,
Sales go up with a hint of disdain.
Penguins sip tea on an ice-capped rock,
Trading gossip that makes others mock.

The rainbows cartwheel, just for show,
While sloths cheer loudly, moving too slow.
In this madness, a spark of bliss,
A couch potato donning a party hat, amiss.

Flowing Dreams in a Summer Breeze

Balloons float high, a sky full of flair,
While sunflowers salsa without a care.
The bees do the cha-cha, buzzing in tune,
As grasshoppers croon to the shining moon.

A picnic blanket full of odd delights,
With cupcakes spinning in whimsical flights.
The ants are in tuxedos, marching in line,
While squirrels debate over who can dine.

Cascading Hues of Quietude

The cloud shapes giggle as they drift away,
A waffle falls in syrup, bright as the day.
Fish in bow ties swim with flair,
Splashing joy like they just don't care.

Pine trees whisper secrets in the breeze,
While chipmunks barter acorns with ease.
A rock band of frogs croak out a tune,
Croaking louder than the crazy moon.

Retreat to Resonance

When waves accuse the sand of theft,
The shells just laugh, they're quite adept.
They know the tide will come and go,
And they'll all dance in ebb and flow.

A crab with shades struts on the shore,
Claiming the beach, he wants much more.
With every splash, he makes a scene,
In this grand show, he's the routine.

Seagulls squawk, like they own the feast,
While munching chips – they're quite the beast.
But as the sun starts to drop low,
They toss a fry, and off they go.

In this retreat where we unwind,
The sand's a friend, so soft and kind.
We'll laugh till stars begin to peak,
In harmony, we find our cheek.

The Fluidity of Calm

A sip of breeze tickles my nose,
As the river winks and mischievously flows.
The ducks are quacking, throwing shade,
At those who think their plans won't fade.

Here comes a fish, with quite the grin,
He jumps and splashes, drawing us in.
In this fluid dance, we all must twirl,
As bubbles rise and the waters swirl.

The sun breaks out, it gleams so bright,
Paddles plop, creating delight.
We sail along with ice cream smiles,
And trade our woes for silly styles.

The evening wraps, a knitted hug,
As laughter echoes like a snug bug.
In this blissful, sprightly flow,
Who knew calm could shine like a show?

Potpourri of Peace

A mix of scents in the ocean air,
With fruity bits tossed without a care.
Salted chips meet tropical punch,
Making waves in our lunchtime crunch.

Yoga on boards, balance is tough,
A splash and a giggle, 'Hey, that's enough!'
We flip and flop, like seals in cheer,
Serenity served with side of beer.

Picnics sprawled, amongst seaweed threads,
Sandwiches wink, while lettuce spreads.
When jelly beans find their way to the mix,
We toast our joys with oceanic tricks.

As night unfurls a velvet sheet,
We light sparklers, making it neat.
In this potpourri of goofy fun,
We celebrate all 'til the day is done.

Ocean's Embrace

The waves dance and swirl with glee,
Seagulls squawk like they're on a spree.
A crab does a jig, what a sight!
Even fish find new moves in the light.

Sandcastles crowned with shells and foam,
The ocean calls, "Come play! Come roam!"
Just watch your shoes, oh, don't get wet,
Or join the crabs in their sunset duet.

Peaceful Horizons

Where the sky meets the sea, what a quest,
Clouds float like cotton, a fluffy nest.
A dolphin pops up, then dives down,
Pretending it's lost, just like a clown.

Sunsets paint the sky with honey,
But don't forget—sand gets funny!
Right on your nose or in your cake,
A grainy surprise that makes you wake.

Serenity's Breath

As the waves whisper secrets so low,
A jellyfish does its slapstick show.
It bounces around, floats like a balloon,
Tickling the toes in a watery tune.

The stars shimmer like sprinkles on pie,
While crabs pull a prank, oh me, oh my!
They wave their claws and strut with flair,
Chasing off worries, without a care.

Lullabies of the Lagoon

In a cozy cove where the breezes glide,
Frogs croak a chorus, full of pride.
With a splash, they leap, in joyous spree,
As a fish flips, laughing, "Look at me!"

The moon's soft glow paints paths of delight,
While otters serenade the sleepy night.
And as you chuckle at their playful sights,
Sleep comes softly, as the lagoon ignites.

Beneath the Surface

Ducks in tuxedos glide with flair,
Waddling past, they comb their hair.
Bubbles rise like jokes so bright,
Splashing laughter in morning light.

Fish in sunglasses share their tales,
Swapping secrets, blowing gales.
Friendship floats on currents strong,
In a world where all belong.

A Symphony of Softness

Clouds compose a fluffy song,
Humming breezes all day long.
The sun strums rays of golden cheer,
While giggles bounce from ear to ear.

Bumblebees dance, doing the jig,
Pollinating joy, oh so big!
Frogs croon croaky lullabies,
As laughter leaps from friendly skies.

The Quilt of Quiet

Stars twinkle in a silent show,
Blanketing dreams that gently flow.
Crickets chirp a silly tune,
Underneath the glowing moon.

Moss soft-cradles sleepy sighs,
While shadows play at midnight's highs.
Whispers float like gentle streams,
Weaving friendship into dreams.

Glimpses of Gentle Grace

A squirrel dons a tiny hat,
As he jitterbugs with a chat.
Bees wear boots, they strut around,
In this funny garden town.

Butterflies laugh, their wings a swirl,
Twisting 'round like they're in a whirl.
Nature's jesters, a comic dance,
In every nook, we find romance.

The Lullaby of Distant Shores

Waves giggle softly, tickling feet,
As seagulls dance, fashionably sweet.
Sandy castles rise, but then they fall,
With shells as crowns, we'll have a ball.

Sunscreen laughter, a slippery mess,
Dancing crabs in their Sunday best.
Ice cream dreams in a waffle cone,
Who knew the ocean could be so prone?

Windswept hair and a silly hat,
Chasing waves, look at that cat!
A seagull swoops with a cheeky surprise,
Stealing our lunch, oh what a prize!

Heartfelt giggles meet the salty air,
With every splash, we shake out our care.
As night falls down with sparkling stars,
We'll toast marshmallows and giggle at jars.

Tranquil Shores and Wandering Hearts

On the beach, where flip-flops roam,
Shells whisper secrets to those who comb.
Footprints dance in the fading light,
As waves play tag with all their might.

Sandy toes and salty jokes,
The ocean's giggle is just for folks.
Kites soar high, a colorful fight,
While crabs wear hats, oh what a sight!

Laughter bubbles like a sunlit stream,
Echoing dreams that make us beam.
With driftwood treasures, we build our lair,
Joking about our wild hair affair!

As twilight whispers its gentle tune,
Stars peep out like a cheeky loon.
Wandering hearts beneath the moon,
Chasing joy, our favorite tune.

Beneath the Veil of Still Waters

Under calm skies, the water's a tease,
As fish throw parties, with giggles and wheeze.
Wishful ducks, they waddle and prance,
In fancy hats, they start to dance.

Lily pads float, a green ballet,
While frogs in tuxedos come out to play.
Sunbeams twinkle, shadows in tow,
As we stretch wide, waiting for the show!

The stillness jokes in a playful way,
Ripples play tag, come join the sway!
With a splash and smile, let's make a mess,
Who knew calm water could be so blessed?

Beneath the tranquil, a lullaby hums,
As right on cue, a soft belly drums.
Joyful moments as we seek the thrills,
In giggly splashes, our laughter spills!

A Symphony of Silent Moments

In quiet corners where shadows blend,
Shells hum a tune that never will end.
Gentle breezes with a playful sigh,
As clouds wear scarves drifting softly by.

Ocean's hush sings a cheeky note,
A silent dance on a dreamy boat.
Laughter floats like a feathered kite,
In secret whispers, hearts feel light.

Pebbles chuckle as they skip and slide,
In forgotten corners, they like to hide.
A mischievous breeze causing mischief in tow,
In every silent moment, our giggles grow.

As day dips down, we gather our tales,
Sailing on dreams, with laughter as sails.
In the symphony where silence plays,
We find our rhythm in the sun's warm rays.

The Canvas of Quiet

In a world of quiet dream,
Where thoughts can fly and gleam,
The ducks waddle with flair,
As they don their silly air.

The trees gossip with leaves,
A chatter that never deceives,
Squirrels on bikes zoom by,
Making everyone laugh and sigh.

Bubbles float in the serene,
Tickling fish beneath the sheen,
With turtles doing the twist,
In this tranquil, blissful mist.

The sun spills laughter each day,
As shadows come out to play,
While clouds wear their cotton hats,
In this land of silly sprats.

Peace in the Layered Depths

Beneath the waves, a party brews,
With crabs in coats and fish in shoes,
The octopus serves snacks that float,
While whales sing in a lively note.

Starfish dance on the sandy floor,
As seahorses twirl, oh, what a score!
Jellyfish laughing in the light,
In the depths where all feels right.

A shark in a tutu does a twirl,
While tiny shrimps have a whirl,
Coral reefs wear a joyful grin,
As bubbly giggles rise and spin.

With every wave, a chuckle's found,
In this goofy underwater ground,
Where peace wears a silly hat,
And the ocean lives in a happy spat.

Gliding into Grace

On a breeze, we dance and glide,
With birds that wear a goofy stride,
Raindrops tap like little feet,
In nature's rhythm, light and sweet.

A bear on roller skates rolls by,
As butterflies buzz in the sky,
The sun shines down, a cheeky spark,
Turning every moment into a lark.

With each spin, a chuckle's born,
As flowers smile from the morn,
The grass wears slippers, comfy, bright,
In this easygoing, joyful flight.

Gliding through laughter and grace,
As clouds drift in a playful race,
Finding calm in silly space,
Where hearts take off without a trace.

Under the Silver Glow

Moonbeams toss a silver line,
As night critters sip their wine,
Fireflies flash their bright fanfare,
In the glow, joy fills the air.

Mice in hats plan a grand feast,
With treats that make the night a beast,
Owls hoot tunes of laughter sweet,
While raccoons tap their dancing feet.

Stars peek down with a wink and grin,
As laughter bubbles from within,
The night unfolds its cozy quilt,
In this place where joy is built.

Underneath the shimmering light,
All worries fade into the night,
With giggles floating on the breeze,
In a world of quirks and ease.

Radiance in Reflection

A fish wore a tie, quite absurd,
It danced on the waves, giving a word.
The seagulls asked, "What's your aim?"
He replied, "Just trying to look tame!"

The sun slipped on water, a slippery ray,
Clam shells clapped, joining the play.
Crabs played marbles with smooth round stones,
While octopuses juggled their hidden bones.

The beach ball floated, dressed like a star,
It rolled into surfers, going too far.
Laughter echoed with every splash,
As jellyfish jived with a bubbling crash.

So here's to the waves, the laughter we share,
With silly antics beyond compare.
The ocean's a stage, under skies so bright,
Where all seems goofy, yet feels just right.

A Haven of Harmony

The seagulls squawked in a wacky tune,
While dolphins joined in with a splashy swoon.
The sandcastles wore crowns of seaweed,
And claimed they were kings in a sandy deed.

A crab danced the cha-cha, what a sight,
With shells for shoes, he twinkled delight.
He waved at the tourists with a grin,
But tripped on a wave, fell flat on his fin.

The beach buddies giggled, sharing a laugh,
As a walrus tried to make a sunbath.
He donned sunglasses, looking quite sly,
But forgot his umbrella, oh my, oh my!

In this joyful realm, with no hint of stress,
Nature's comedy brings pure success.
With every heart full of silly charm,
Peace blooms here, in this quirky farm.

Texture of Tranquility

A jellyfish wobbled with flair so bold,
In underwater dance, shiny and gold.
He bumped into a clam, who just said, "Hey!"
"Watch where you're flapping, you're ruining my day!"

Sand pipers ran races, tiny and fast,
Playing tag with the winds, what a blast!
They whirled and twirled on the soft, warm sand,
Chasing their shadows, a scattered band.

Meanwhile, a pelican, sporting a hat,
Tried to catch fish but ended up flat.
An octopus laughed and snapped a quick pic,
Of the pelican's flop, just a humorous trick.

So let the waves roll, bring giggles and cheer,
As laughter and joy fill up the pier.
In moments of silliness, peace takes flight,
Carried on ripples of pure delight.

Beyond the Mist

There's a porpoise with a bubble machine,
Making the ocean a sparkling scene.
He laughed with the seaweed, waving hello,
While crabs did the limbo, all in a row.

In a fog, there appeared a funny sight,
A shark wearing glasses, what a delight!
He read a book, but it slipped from his grip,
He tossed it to shore in a hilarious flip.

The turtles grooved to the rhythm so sweet,
Bringing joy to the sand with their two left feet.
They twirled in the sand, under soft glowing light,
Turning the sea into a dance floor tonight.

So here's to the laughter, the moments we find,
In the waves and the calm, we leave worries behind.
With giggles and fun, our hearts stay in tune,
As we float in the joy, beneath the bright moon.

The Beauty of Calm After the Storm.

The sky is clear, the sun's a clown,
Silly clouds wear a funny gown.
Waves giggle as they brush the shore,
Laughing at storms; they shout, 'No more!'

Seagulls dance, they prance in air,
With flapping wings, they show off flair.
A crab does the cha-cha on the sand,
While fish tell jokes; isn't life grand?

Children splash with laughter loud,
Creating waves, they make us proud.
The ocean grins, its surface gleams,
In this moment, we float on dreams.

Whispers of Serenity

Breezes play, they tickle the trees,
Whispering secrets, carried with ease.
A cat on a log, with a curious stare,
Looks like it's plotting, oh, what a dare!

The frogs croak jokes, a hilarious scene,
In the pond where the waters gleam.
A turtle giggles, it's quite aware,
That slow and steady wins the funny hair!

Fish flip-flop, starting a race,
Their underwater antics a comical chase.
Clouds shape-shift into furry beasts,
Nature's humor never seems to cease.

Currents of Calm

Under the sun, all seems so bright,
Even the shadows are feeling light.
A lone otter floats by with grace,
Sporting a hat, oh what a face!

The river dances, it wiggles and sways,
While frogs play poker in clever ways.
A fish tips its hat, just for a laugh,
This tranquil water's a funny craft!

Bubbles rise, like giggles in air,
The trees sway softly, without a care.
A squirrel with style steals the show,
In these calm waters, fun seems to flow.

Embrace of Still Waters

A still pond lies like glass, so bright,
Reflections chuckle in morning light.
A duck quacks jokes, don't take it to heart,
For laughter's the reason, it plays its part.

The lilies nod with a cheeky grin,
As if they know where the fun begins.
A fish flips a coin; what luck it brings,
Wishing for laughter as the water sings!

Sunbeams dance on the surface fine,
Casting sparkles like sweetened wine.
In the embrace of these calm scenes,
Life's funny quirks dance like daydreams.

Heartbeats of Harmony

In a cradle of waves, the seagulls hum,
While jellyfish dance, looking quite dumb.
The starfish lounge in their carefree glee,
Waving to fish who swim off in a spree.

The crabs hold a meeting, a council of sand,
Discussing the best way to form a band.
With shells for the drums and seaweed for strings,
They jam by the shores; laughter surely rings.

A clam thinks it's wise, offers pearls for free,
But all of his friends just roll with the sea.
For life under waves is a comedy show,
Where bubbles of laughter just float to and fro.

So when the sun sets, and the sea turns to gold,
The ocean's secrets are playfully told.
With giggles of waves, and chuckles from shells,
The humor of nature in rhythm compels.

Tranquil Reflections

A pond filled with frogs, croaking in style,
They leap in a chorus, making you smile.
The lilies are watching with a knowing nod,
While turtles ponder life, feeling quite odd.

The dragonflies zoom like they're racing a train,
While a fish swims by, wearing a grin like a bane.
The sun's shiny rays make the ripples engage,
In a dance of reflections, they take center stage.

The otters slide down from their slippery throne,
Splashing all round, they dive for a bone.
The ducks, quite annoyed, quack a loud cheer,
As the merry-go-round of the pond draws near.

So raise up your glass, let the laughter commence,
For nature's a jester, with humor immense.
Reflecting on joy in the water's embrace,
A gathering spot for a giggling race.

Murmurs of the Bay

The breeze tells a story in whispers and sighs,
While pelicans take off, soaring through the skies.
The shells gather closely, gossiping low,
About crabs on the run, putting on quite a show.

A fish yells out, "Hey, watch me glide!"
But tangled in nets, he tries to hide.
The shore birds all chuckle, they know a good trick,
In the realm of the sea, life's a comedic flick.

The waves play tag with the rocks and the sand,
While a whale tries to wiggle, it doesn't go as planned.
With a splash and a laugh, he sends fish a-flying,
In the theater of water, there's never a crying.

So join in the giggles, let worries set sail,
For the bay is alive with a humorous tale.
Its whispers bring joy, softly tickling the air,
In the place where the sea and laughter can share.

Quiet Waters Run Deep

In still waters resting, the frogs are on cue,
Croaking their wisdom, both old and new.
With skip and a splash, they leap with delight,
Imitating stars, twinkling in the night.

The turtles are wise, but they take their time,
Moving like they're lost, yet in perfect rhyme.
The kingfisher swoops, in search of a meal,
But watching his antics, is part of the deal.

As ripples form circles, the fish play charades,
Performing great dives in synchronized parades.
Their scales glimmer bright, like a disco ball,
In the quiet of waters, nature's behind-the-wall.

So sip from the stillness, let laughter pour out,
Embrace every moment, there's no need to pout.
For in the calm depths of life's playful sweep,
We find that the stillest of waters can leap.

Serenity's Embrace

In silliness we find our grace,
With jellyfish in their jelly race.
Seagulls laugh in the salty air,
While crabs do their dance without a care.

A turtle swims in a cowboy hat,
Singing songs of a sleepy cat.
The ocean chuckles, waves do sway,
Creating giggles throughout the day.

Underneath the moon's glow bright,
A sea star twirls with sheer delight.
Shells conspire in a funny chat,
While dolphins leap and greet the spat.

With friends on shore, we sip some tea,
As fish throw parties under the sea.
In this embrace, we shall remain,
Where laughs and joy wash away the pain.

Whispering Waves of Tranquility

Waves whisper tales like giggling nuns,
Telling stories of swimming puns.
The fish all wear their finest ties,
As crabs play chess while others rise.

Seagulls mime a sneaky trick,
As sandy toes play hide and pick.
A starfish dreams of a cabaret,
While seaweed sways in a lively ballet.

Octopuses juggle with shiny shells,
While clams gossip in huddled swells.
The sun slides down, painting the bay,
A comical end to a joyous day.

With a splash, a surfboard flies,
Landing straight on an unwatched prize.
Laughter erupts from land to tide,
For in this dance, all woes subside.

The Calm Before the Dawn

Beneath the stars, the fun begins,
Where sea critters all wear fins.
A walrus sings in a deep, loud voice,
As sea cucumbers cheer, rejoice!

The fish flip-flop in fancy shoes,
Playing pranks like ocean blues.
With dolphins racing, they shout hooray,
While jellyfish wave in a joyful fray.

As morning breaks, a sea lion yawns,
With sleepy eyes and flip-flop pawns.
Squirting water, a whale joins in,
Making waves with a toothy grin.

In this lull, laughter fills the air,
As all sea creatures join to share.
The calm before the dawn's bright glow,
Is filled with joy, as smiles overflow.

Soft Echoes on the Shore

On sandy banks, laughter sparkles,
As crabs wear shades and do their rambles.
Seashells gossip like old maids,
While fish draw lines in surface shades.

A pelican mimes a grand old show,
Dancing with flippers, stealing the glow.
The waves break softly with a hush,
As seagulls join in a feathered rush.

The tide brings in tales woven tight,
Of underwater pranks in the night.
With flip-flops flung and hats aflight,
Everything feels just incredibly right.

As the sun dips low, the sky does gleam,
We laugh and dance, in a joyous dream.
Soft echoes whisper through the night,
Where funny tales find their purest light.

Celestial Calmness

Beneath the stars, a cat does nap,
While dreams take flight, a gentle flap.
The moon wears shades, so cool, so bright,
And giggles softly, 'What a sight!'

An owl hoots jokes from yonder tree,
As squirrels laugh in harmony.
The breeze replies with tickled sighs,
While fireflies dance, a bright surprise.

The world's so chill, it's hard to frown,
Even the dog wears a crown!
He barks with glee at clouds up high,
And winks at fish that swim on by.

So let's enjoy this cosmic clown,
Where laughter grows and never drowns.
In this vast space where joy does swell,
Even the stars have tales to tell.

Reflections in Stillness

A pond so clear, it holds a grin,
Reflections show the world within.
A frog jumps high, lands with a plop,
And ducks parade, can't make it stop!

The sun throws rays like playful darts,
While fish share their caustic smarts.
They splash around, quite full of glee,
Claiming they're better at hide and see.

A ladybug dons a stylish hat,
Admonishing flies for being fat.
She dances round, on water's skin,
While dragonflies giggle, "Shall we spin?"

So watch the fun, don't miss the view,
In this stillness, joy feels new.
With every ripple, laughter we hear,
Nature's jesters, wildly sincere!

The Dance of Gentle Breezes

The breezes swirl, a playful tease,
Whispers secrets through the trees.
With every gust, a leaf takes flight,
A drunken twirl, it's quite a sight!

A butterfly flits with silly grace,
Chasing shadows, it's in the race.
No one can land, it's pure delight,
As nature spins this waltzing night.

The grasses sway, they join the fun,
Shaking hands with the setting sun.
A picnic blanket does a jig,
And ants are boogying their own gig!

So let the breezes lift your soul,
Join in the dance, that's the goal.
With laughter echoing in the air,
There's joy found everywhere!

Serene Moments at Dusk

Dusk arrives with hues so bold,
A canvas painted, tales unfold.
The crickets start their nightly sing,
As fireflies light the buzzing fling.

The sky's a buffet, colors collide,
As day and night take a fun ride.
A raccoon giggles at his reflection,
While stars align in a grand connection.

A breeze whispers puns, a subtle jest,
For night time reveals the joyous best.
The moon brings popcorn, sharing with glee,
"Let's watch the night like a movie!"

So as the sun bids sweet goodbye,
Fill your heart, let laughter fly.
For in these moments, light and free,
The world's a stage of silly spree!

Embracing the Evening

As the sun slips, ducks start to quack,
Evening snacks disappear from the sack.
Laughter spills like tea on the floor,
Who knew sunsets could make us snore?

The moon winks down, quite the prank,
Stars in pajamas, they're all quite drank.
Crickets sing like they've lost their notes,
While fireflies dance in their little boats.

Fish jump high, a silly ballet,
Sardines whisper, 'Let's swim away!'
The breeze tries to pull off a joke,
But it's the trees that truly provoke.

Finally night wraps us all tight,
Dreams chuckle softly, a giggly flight.
As we slip into slumber's embrace,
We hear tomorrow will join the grace.

Elysian Echoes

Whispering winds play a tune of cheer,
Clouds puff up and giggle near.
Lemonade rivers flow with a grin,
Silly fish join in the spin.

Mountains wear glasses, looking quite wise,
While valleys hide, covered in pies.
Bees buzz jokes that tickle the air,
In a world where laughter has no compare.

Sunflowers dance like nobody's watching,
Grass blades wiggle, oh so fetching.
Rain drops join in, making a splash,
Grinning as puddles begin to clash.

Dreamy whispers float through the night,
Creatures in pajamas bask in the light.
In this mirthful echo, we're all free,
Where humor and joy blend like a sea.

Flowing with the Silence

On a quiet lake, ducks put on a show,
Rowing their boats, moving slow.
Ripples giggle as the fish take flight,
Even the stones try to dance tonight.

Clouds joke above, draping down fluff,
While shadows twist, they've had enough.
A turtle whispers secrets of fate,
While trees chuckle, it's never too late.

Stillness wraps round like a warm hug,
And giggles bubble in each snug bug.
The sun throws paint on the calm parade,
As laughter blooms in the light cascade.

So let's flow with the silence, take a leap,
In this quirky dream, where giggles creep.
Through the night's canvas, we glide and sing,
In the quiet moments, joy takes wing.

Still Waters

In the stillness, frogs wear tiny hats,
Bouncing on lily pads, making chitchats.
The sun sets low with a playful wink,
As the ducks discuss their favorite drink.

Mirrors of water reflect the fun,
Fish crack jokes till the day is done.
Ripples play tag with the evening breeze,
While ants throw a party amongst the trees.

Silently, stars attend the feast,
While a cricket performs, to say the least.
Nearby, the moon wears a crown of cheese,
'Tis a night of giggles and whims that tease.

So here's to stillness, a laugh-filled night,
Where nature's humor takes to flight.
In every shadow, a chuckle hides,
This quiet magic in light abides.

Soft Dreams

As night descends, the blanket unfolds,
Pillows giggle, they've got stories untold.
Moonlight swirls with a twist of fun,
Dreams bring laughter 'til the day is done.

Clouds lay down, all fluffy and bright,
Feathers tickle as stars wink goodnight.
Bunnies bounce through the moonbeams,
Chasing the whispers of nightly dreams.

In the garden, shadows start to dance,
As playful breeze leads a happy prance.
Everything hums soft lullabies,
With giggles wrapped in the deep blue skies.

So drift away to this enchanting land,
Where joy and silliness go hand in hand.
As soft dreams roam, don't hold them tight,
For they sprinkle laughter till morning light.

The Stillness Beneath

In the calm of a pond, I skated with glee,
A fish waved goodbye, he wanted his tea.
I giggled so hard, but slipped on a shoe,
With a splash and a plop, my trousers turned blue.

A frog croaked a joke, ribbit-ribbit hooray!
He said, "That's okay, I was hopping today!"
We laughed 'til we rolled, our bellies did ache,
In the stillness, there's chaos, just look for the wake.

The sunbeams decided to dance on my nose,
While geese in a row honked, posing like pros.
The breeze told a riddle, the trees joined the game,
It turns out the woodpecker's really to blame!

So if you find stillness in laughter and play,
Just look for the puddles where mischief can stay.
Peace hides in the silliness, joy's in the strife,
And the frogs with their jokes make chaos feel nice.

Echoes of Quietude

A whispering breeze brushed my cheek, oh so light,
It tickled my nose, making me giggle outright.
The clouds started chuckling, oh what a sight!
As squirrels held a meeting, debating the night.

I spotted a turtle, he wore tiny shades,
He claimed he was fast, but only in spades.
"The world's just too swift, I just can't keep pace,"
But he grinned while munching on a leaf of lace.

The sun took a nap, all the shadows got spun,
Even old Mister Owl joined in for some fun.
"Whooo cares?" he hooted, with a wink and a flap,
In the echoes of quietude, who needs a map?

So here in the silence, where laughter can bloom,
We question the quiet, we giggle, we zoom.
In shadows of whispers, a ruckus can cease,
And all of life's antics, they gather our peace.

A Harbor of Harmony

At the dock, I met fish with sunglasses so cool,
They grinned and they splashed, making waves in the pool.
A crab played some tunes on a conch by the shore,
While seagulls were dancing, who could ask for more?

A boat with a parrot, so bright and so loud,
Said, "Join me for crackers; let's gather a crowd!"
The waves whispered secrets only sailors would know,
As the tide turned to laughter, in the sunshine's glow.

We all shared our stories, both silly and wise,
A dolphin cracked jokes, much to our surprise.
In this harbor of harmony, with friends all around,
Even barnacles chuckled, it was quite the sound!

So come join the fun, let's raise our cheer high,
In the boat of good humor, together we fly.
With each splash we make, in the laughter we sail,
In this harbor of joy, may peace always prevail.

Driftwood Dreams

On a beach where driftwood loves to recline,
I met a few shells, they were sipping on brine.
They told me sweet stories of waves far away,
While a starfish took notes, "I'm starting a play!"

The sand was a stage as the crabs pranced around,
With a mermaid on drums, they rocked the whole ground.

The sun beamed with laughter, painting skies bold,
Where seagulls made magic, with tales they had told.

I dreamed up a world where all critters danced,
Where jellyfish giggled, and each sea creature pranced.
The currents sang softly, with jokes from the deep,
While the moonflower opened, its secrets to keep.

So here on this shoreline, with driftwood aglow,
We find peace in the laughter, it's a beautiful show.
With dreams in the sand and smiles in each wave,
In the ocean's embrace, we all feel so brave.

Waves of Tranquility

The ocean whispers, 'Hey there, friend,'
As seagulls laugh and the fishes pretend.
A crab does a dance, with two left feet,
While surfers giggle, falling in their seat.

The sun shines bright, a golden light,
Splashing the beach with pure delight.
A sandcastle stands, proud, unreal,
Until a wave comes in for the steal.

Seashells wear hats made of seaweed fine,
Each one a story, a jester's line.
With every splash, the giggles flow,
The secrets of peace in the undertow.

So let's chase bubbles as they float by,
And watch the clouds that dance in the sky.
With laughter as vast as the ocean blue,
We'll find our joy in the playful view.

Soft Shores of Solace

At the shoreline, where silliness reigns,
A dog digs deep, ignoring the pains.
With every flop and every roll,
It buries its problems in a sandy hole.

Here, flip-flops fling in the breeze so wild,
As children giggle, each foot a mile.
A seagull swoops for a chip—oh wait!
The human yells back, 'That's my dinner plate!'

The waves whisper jokes in a bubbly tone,
While jellyfish drift with a grace all their own.
A sandpiper struts on its tiny parade,
Each step a punchline, each dance a charade.

So grab your pail and your shoveling spoon,
Let's build a weird castle under the moon.
With laughter and light on this soft, sunny shore,
We'll wave at our lives, begging for more.

Harmony in the Horizon

In the distance, the horizon grins,
Where the sky meets the sea, and fun begins.
With a wink of the sun and a splash of a wave,
Even the fish pipe up, 'We're all very brave!'

A sailboat giggles, tipping its hat,
While the wind tells tales about a friendly cat.
The clouds compete to tell the best tale,
Of mermaid parties and snail races by sail.

On piers of laughter, fishermen joke,
Of fish that whispered, of seaweed folk.
With each cast line, a chuckle ensues,
As they reel in their dreams, not just the blues.

With the sun setting low, turning gold into pink,
The waves join the chorus, making us think.
In this land of chuckles, where joys align,
We find harmony in laughter, oh how divine!

Gentle Ripples of Hope

Watch as ripples dance with a silly cheer,
Each one a tickle, a joy to the ear.
A frog jumps in, causing quite the splash,
While turtles roll by, moving slow with panache.

The lily pads giggle, wearing crowns of dew,
As dragonflies flutter, in colors so new.
'Who knew serenity could be such a hoot?'
As a fish pops its head up, wearing a suit.

Bubbles rise up, with secrets to share,
Telling tales of splashes, love, and the fair.
The sun winks down on this watery stage,
With laughter and hope at each rippling page.

So let's join the dance in this blissful space,
As joy floats around, a soft, warm embrace.
In these gentle ripples, we'll find what we seek,
A universe giggling, along with the creek.

Moonlit Waters

The moon took a dip in the ocean's embrace,
Giggling fish splashed, declaring their grace.
Stars joined the party, twinkling with glee,
A crab on the shore danced—look, it's for me!

The waves told secrets, but laughed out of turn,
A jellyfish joking, said, 'Watch how I churn!'
Seagulls onlookers, they cawed and they cheered,
In this watery circus, no one ever feared.

Seaweed did the limbo, the starfish clapped hands,
Even the plankton joined in the bands.
Bubbles were popping like jokes on the line,
As the ocean chuckled, 'This life is divine!'

At dawn every creature returned to their beds,
With dreams filled with laughter, soft pillows for heads.
The tide rolled back gently, waves bid their farewell,
'We'll see you next night for more stories to tell!'

Sanctuary in Silence

In a quiet nook where crickets conspire,
A frog found a throne, he sings to inspire.
Toads joined the chorus, all strict with their tones,
While ants in the background danced with their phones.

Bees buzzing softly, exclaimed, 'What a scene!'
They sipped on sweet nectar, it's like a caffeine.
Grasshoppers laughed as they twirled with the breeze,
'Who knew such a spot could put us at ease?'

In this silent haven, the laughter rang loud,
When squirrels told tales of the nutty old crowd.
A cake made of leaves was shared without fuss,
While the wise old owl said, 'Now, that's a plus!'

But as day turned to night, they packed their delight,
With promises made to return by moonlight.
In the sanctuary's warmth, they shared one last grin,
Until next time, friends, let the fun times begin!

Wandering in Whispered Paths

Through leafy trails where whispers reside,
A snail told a tale, his shell filled with pride.
The path was a riddle, but no one was lost,
With laughter as currency, they paid no cost.

A raccoon with sunglasses declared it a stroll,
His sidekick, a mouse, did a dance on a pole.
The trees all leaned in, ears perked up to hear,
As shadows grew playful, spreading good cheer.

Mushrooms giggled shyly as dancers passed by,
Offering snacks that produced a loud sigh.
'Not for your toes!' teased a squirrel in a hat,
And everyone burst out in a fit of 'What's that?'

As dusk painted colors across the soft sky,
They waved their goodbyes to each passerby.
In their hearts, a promise to wander anew,
On the whispered paths where the laughter just grew.

The Essence of Equanimity

On a sunny hill where the daisies unite,
A turtle said, 'Slowly, everything's right.'
While rabbits raced circles, all frantic and fast,
The turtle sat still, saying, 'Peace is a blast!'

Bees buzzing freely, always in flight,
Declared he was weird for keeping it light.
'You're missing the point!' chirped a wise old crow,
'It's not about speed; it's about how you flow!'

The sun made a joke, brushing clouds on the side,
While shadows danced lightly with graciously pride.
Every creature nodded, they smiled and then said,
'Finding calm in chaos is truly widespread!'

So with each gentle breeze that brought laughter anew,
They wove a bright tapestry of moments so true.
In the essence of balance, they learned to embrace,
That life is a journey, a joyful, sweet race!

A Canvas of Softest Blues

Upon the shore, a crab did dance,
Wiggling sideways in its silly prance.
Seagulls giggle, chasing their fate,
While waves whisper jokes, not quite first-rate.

Flip-flops fling from hapless toes,
As sunscreens squirt in crazy flows.
Buckets and spades in a wacky race,
Who knew that sand could bring such grace?

A starfish grins, its arms out wide,
"I'm not a fish! Just sunbathe with pride!"
Shells chuckle softly beneath the tide,
In this beach life, pure joy won't hide.

As ice cream melts in the summer heat,
Jokes swim around on playful feet.
With sandy hair and laughter bright,
Who cares about wrong when it feels so right?

The Haven of Sweet Respite

In a hammock strung between two trees,
A squirrel swings, "This life's a breeze!"
Lemonade sips bring giggles and cheers,
While flies attempt their dance of peers.

A napkin flies, caught in the breeze,
"Catch me if you can!" it taunts with ease.
Mismatched socks on a sunbaked lawn,
Playful shenanigans are never gone.

Bubbles arise from a nearby pond,
"Blow me bigger, make me fond!"
Frogs croak laughter, a jolly tune,
Dancing together beneath the moon.

Time twists gently in this laid-back space,
Where worries vanish without a trace.
In a haven that nudges joy to stay,
Life becomes a game; let's laugh and play!

Rugged Cliffs and Gentle Winds

On rugged cliffs where brave men bumble,
Waves chuckle below, delight in the tumble.
Rocky paths lead to not-so-great feels,
"Don't trip!" shout the seagulls, "We're not with wheels!"

Daredevils shout from heights with glee,
"I'm the captain of my own 'crazy' sea!"
Wind whips through hair, wild as a tune,
Chasing off clouds and a looming monsoon.

A picnic basket rolls away, oh dear,
Grapes playing tag, "Catch us if you're near!"
Cheese takes a tumble with crackers in tow,
While ants plot mischief in a well-rehearsed show.

As day turns to night, laughter echoes free,
With jesters in hats, all dancing with glee.
Adventure calls forth with every gust,
In this rugged embrace, we simply must trust!

Echoes of Stillness in the Night

Under the stars, the crickets compose,
A symphony sweet, with schtick and some prose.
"Do you hear that?" a firefly winks,
As night wraps around us in soft, gentle blinks.

The moon grins wide, a joker in sight,
Casting funny shadows that dance in delight.
With marshmallows roasted, and giggles abound,
In this tranquil madness, pure joy knows no bounds.

A raccoon appears, with mischief on mind,
Stealing snacks like it's blissfully blind.
"Was that yours?" it shrugs with a grin,
In the dark, it finds treasures should startles begin.

Stillness giggles, while we drift away,
Wrapped in the echoes where shadows play.
With dreams of laughter lighting the night,
In this cozy sphere, everything feels right.

Nature's Gentle Whisper

The breeze tickles leaves, they giggle with glee,
A squirrel's audition for a tree's comedy.
Sunbeams play tag, hiding under the shade,
I swear, the daisies just joined a parade!

The pond is a stage for ducks in a row,
Quacking their jokes, but it's hard not to flow.
Frogs leap with flair in their green little suits,
While fish trade their puns like a couple of brutes.

Clouds are the audience, drifting in fashion,
Each giggle of nature is met with a splashin'.
Laughter erupts like a tune in the air,
World's greatest show, if you just stop and stare!

So let's dance with the wind, and wiggle like worms,
Life's little nuggets, they come with some squirms.
Nature's a joker with a smile in its eyes,
In this funny world, madness wears a disguise.

The Heart of Calm

In a hammock so cozy, I nap through the day,
While ants start a conga, they wiggle and sway.
A butterfly flutters, wearing a bright tie,
With a wink and a flutter, it waves me goodbye.

The sun's just a cartoon with a silly grin,
It paints the horizon, where giggles begin.
Chirping with zeal, the crickets conspire,
Each joke they create, sets the night on fire.

Down by the river, the fish tell a joke,
"Why did the turtle cross? Just to provoke!"
Laughter bounces back like a rubbery ball,
As even the willows just chuckle and call.

So float in this moment, let worries all cease,
With nature on stage, it's a marvelous feast.
In a realm of delight, find your inner charm,
For life's just a jest, wrapped in nature's arm.

The Harmony of Horizons

Seagulls bore witness to a jest at the shore,
While crabs gather 'round, looking for an encore.
The waves play a tune, they frolic and prance,
Each splash a reminder of nature's great dance.

Dolphins do flips, with a wink and a cheer,
Trading seaweed for jokes that are hard to hear.
The horizon's a canvas, painted blue and bright,
As laughter spills forth like stars in the night.

Shells form a circus—sands fill the seats,
With clams telling stories while seahorses tweet.
Each grain has a tale, old folks share a grin,
As tides play their jokes, let hilarity in.

So let's wade in the silliness, dance with the tide,
In harmony's arms, we'll take life in stride.
With sea breezes tickling, let laughter arise,
For laughter's the treasure, pain's but a disguise.

Somewhere in Stillness

In the shade of a tree, the world takes a pause,
With bees making music, they've earned some applause.
A snail on a mission, takes life nice and slow,
"Why dash through the grass when you've got all the flow?"

Among the soft flowers, the butterflies twirl,
Spreading their giggles like sweet candy swirl.
The breeze tickles petals, oh what a delight,
Like nature's own whispers that giggle at night.

Crickets provide rhythm, a quirky band there,
With frogs as the dancers, we laugh without care.
The calmness around us is filled up with fun,
As life's simple moments make laughter outrun.

So let go of the hurry, just linger awhile,
In stillness, find joy that brings forth a smile.
For each tiny creature has tales to convey,
With humor in nature, who needs disarray?

Celestial Peace

In the sky, the clouds do dance,
While birds wear hats, take a chance.
Stars giggle at the moon's bright light,
Even the sun is feeling quite polite.

Waves crash but have a funny twist,
They've got rhythm, can't resist.
Fish in tuxedos swim with flair,
Making waves without a care.

Comets down, with smiles they glide,
Bumping into rocks, with nowhere to hide.
The cosmos chuckles, so full of cheer,
As planets join in, perfection near.

Galaxies swirl in a happy whirl,
Spinning tales, giving life a twirl.
Peace, it seems, has quite the laugh,
In this cosmic comedy of the celestial half.

The Language of Stillness

In a meadow, crickets make a fuss,
Chirping secrets, causing a bus.
Butterflies wear glasses, it's quite absurd,
Joining the talk, but barely heard.

Trees hold conferences, leaves vote on sway,
Debating the best ways to play.
"Let's whisper," one says with a grin,
"Then no one will hear the fun we're in!"

Rabbits hop, discussing the moon,
"Should we hop fast or sing a tune?"
Squirrels simply munch on nuts,
Laughing as they dodge the cuts.

Peace lingers here, under the sun,
Chasing away what's not fun.
With every chuckle, the stillness grows,
In the language of laughter, anything goes!

Serenity's Kiss

A soft breeze tickles the daisies' hair,
While bees wear boots, what a silly affair!
Clouds whisper secrets, they paint the skies,
Wishing for ice cream in every size.

Ducks waddle by, quacking out puns,
While frogs in bow ties practice their runs.
Sunbeams giggle, they tickle the lake,
Making ripples for laughter's sake.

The mountains snicker, their peaks so high,
Sharing jokes with the passing sky.
Stars bling their smiles, twinkling bright,
In the stillness of the giggling night.

Amidst all the joy, serenity glows,
Kissing each moment, as laughter flows.
It's a funny world when peace plays its part,
Where smiles and silence fill every heart.

Ripples of Reverie

In the pond, the frogs put on a show,
Jumping for joy, making quite a row.
Their echoes ripple oh so wide,
While fish in wigs just swim with pride.

Marshmallows float, a sweet little fate,
Silly dreams dance upon a plate.
The water reflects a laugh so true,
Every bubble carries a giggle or two.

Imaginations fly like kites in the air,
Tickling the wind without a care.
Giggling moose strut by the shore,
While otters perform, wanting an encore.

In this flow of whimsical cheer,
Ripples of joy draw us near.
As laughter echoes in gentle streams,
Peace finds a home in our funniest dreams.

The Sounds of Serenity's Melody

The gulls squawk loud, like they own the sky,
While fish jump up, with a flippy high.
The waves clap hands, a watery cheer,
Bubbles rise up, like they have no fear.

The boats bob along, in a dance of their own,
While crabs in the sand, make a little throne.
Seaweed wiggles, in an ocean jig,
Silly sea creatures, all big and gig.

A seal plays peek-a-boo, with a twist and a turn,
While starfish lounge, waiting for their turn.
The sun gets comfy, on the horizon wide,
With a wink and a grin, it starts to slide.

So let's grab our buckets, for a sandy spree,
Building castles with laughter, just you and me.
With the ocean's tune, we'll dance on the shore,
While the world around giggles, wanting more!

Unwritten Stories Beneath the Stars

Under the sky, with twinkling eyes,
We sketch out tales, as the owl flies.
Each star a dot, in our cosmic game,
Whispering secrets, as they call our names.

A crab tells a joke, with a pun on his shell,
While fishes gossip, it's a splashy carousel.
The moon joins in, with a light-hearted grin,
While comets race by, inviting us in.

We catch playful breezes, that swish through the night,
As fireflies twinkle, like a sparkly light.
With laughter like waves, we swirl and spin,
Our unwritten stories, now ready to begin.

So let's make a pact, to laugh till we snore,
Under the stars, oh, what fun is in store!
With each little chuckle, we'll etch in the dark,
A tale of joy, where dreams leave a mark!

Moments of Stillness at Water's Edge

At the water's rim, we watch the show,
As sea foam fluffs in an endless flow.
A paddleboard flamingo, a sight quite absurd,
As kids in the waves shout, 'Let's fly like a bird!'

Seagulls plot heists on unseen french fries,
While sandy toes wiggle, much to their surprise.
The sun takes a dip, like it's checking the tide,
While beach balls rally, in a joyous glide.

The hermit crabs march, in a little parade,
Wearing shells of the finest, in hues that won't fade.
With laughter in the air, on this sandy retreat,
Life's little moments feel quite the treat.

So let's linger a while, at nature's quaint edge,
With smiles and tickles, let's make a pledge.
To savor the stillness, where giggles unite,
In this goofy sanctuary, all day and all night.

Soft Sands and Silvered Reflections

As soft as a whisper, the sand hugs our toes,
With footprints that giggle, wherever it goes.
Pebbles gossip cheerfully, in a short, chippy speech,
While the ocean chuckles, on it they leech.

Silver waves shimmer, like a sparkly dance,
While we roll on the beach, giving life a chance.
A crab tries to cha-cha, with two left feet,
While the sea turtles bob, in their slow little beat.

The sunset paints laughter, in shades of bright gold,
With stories unfolding, like a tale to be told.
Shells wear their colors, as they prance on the shore,
Each one a treasure, that begs us for more.

So we gather our stories, in soft, sandy bear hugs,
Capturing moments, like tiny little jugs.
With the laughter of waves, echoing our way,
We'll treasure these whims, come what may!

Sanctum of Shimmering Dreams

In a land where jellybeans grow,
And flowers play peek-a-boo,
I found a chair made of marshmallows,
Where no one wears a shoe!

Clouds wear hats, very silly hats,
They float by with a grin,
Sipping tea with a dancing cat,
And that's where fun begins!

Giggles drift like bubbles high,
In a breeze of chocolate rain,
Laughter bounces, oh my oh my,
It just might drive you insane!

So dance with worms in polka dots,
And twirl with gnomes in the sun,
In this haven of melting spots,
Where every day is pure fun!

The Melody of Mellow Days

The sun plays tunes on mangos sweet,
While fish wear tiny shoes,
Dancing under rhythmic beats,
Would you care to join the hues?

Squirrels play the tambourine,
And turtles strum guitars,
Each note a feathered dream,
Underneath the twinkling stars.

Nomadic clouds roll on the floor,
Bouncing like a lively hare,
As giggles open every door,
Can you feel the joy in the air?

Join the fun on this mellow ride,
With candy-cane confetti,
Let laughter be your joyful guide,
As you feel light and petty!

Driftwood Reveries

On driftwood boats with sail of cheese,
We cruise through jelly oceans,
With giggles carried on the breeze,
And laughter's joyful motions.

The fish wear hats made out of pie,
As dolphins dance and cheer,
They've got a party in the sky,
You ought to bring some beer!

With every wave, a joke's been cast,
Like shadows chasing sun,
The seagulls giggle, having a blast,
Oh, this is silly fun!

So grab a slice of cloud-shaped cake,
And join the merry crew,
In swirling dreams, our hearts awake,
Where laughter is the glue!

Landscapes of Light

In a world where shadows skip and twirl,
And sunlight tickles the grass,
Rainbow pigeons dance and swirl,
Time flies like a wobbly lass!

Giant cupcakes grow on trees,
And rivers flow with fizz,
Where every laugh is sure to please,
And joy is what it is!

Butterflies play peek-a-boo,
With bees in funny coats,
Their zany antics, tried and true,
Make us all break into hoats!

So wander through this gleeful place,
Where fun is the theme and rhyme,
Each day is filled with happy grace,
In a land that dances with time!

Embracing Stillness Under Moonlight

In the night, the stars do dance,
My cat thinks it's a chance,
To chase those lights across the sky,
While I sit here wondering why.

The moon laughs with a silvery grin,
As I dodge my neighbor's chicken skin,
Crickets chirp their secret tune,
While I sip on my cold maroon.

The breeze whispers a silly joke,
As I trip over my own cloak,
Yet in this chaos, peace is found,
In every laugh, sweet joy surrounds.

So here I sit, beneath the glow,
Where awkward moments gently flow,
Each giggle serenades the night,
In stillness wrapped, the world feels right.

Flowing Harmony of the Soul

A squirrel scurries with a nut,
While I ponder why I strut,
My mismatched socks begin to sing,
Wishing it were cooler, like spring.

The trees sway in a funky beat,
As I shuffle on my two left feet,
Nature's concert, a silly scene,
With bees buzzing like a tambourine.

The river giggles, splashes bright,
As fish tease me, quite a sight,
Every ripple an amusing dance,
Inviting me to take a chance.

In this flow, no rules apply,
As I toss worries to the sky,
With laughter's echo in my chest,
Each moment here feels like a jest.

The Gentle Rhythm of Solitude

In solitude, I trip and fumble,
With thoughts that giggle and tumble,
A bird throws shade on my sweet tea,
As if it knows, just wait and see.

The clock ticks a silly song,
While I dance where I belong,
Each second feels like a good pun,
Time flies when you're having fun!

My shadow joins the jovial jig,
As I wave to a passing pig,
A breeze of laughter fills the air,
In this solitude, none compare.

So here I spin, a joyful spree,
In gentle rhythm, just me and me,
A giggle here, a snort there too,
In this alone state, bliss blooms anew.

Where Silence Meets the Sea

At the shore where silence reigns,
I witness turtles in funny chains,
As they race towards the bright blue,
I cheer them on, "You can do two!"

The waves clap like an audience row,
While my sandcastle wobbles, oh no!
Seagulls squawk, they're part of the act,
As I find my shovel, a trusty pact.

A crab sidesteps with rhythmic flair,
While I try to tame my wild hair,
The sea's laughter sprays like confetti,
In moments like this, life feels ready.

So, here I sit, where silence speaks,
Embracing giggles, not just peaks,
In the waves' ebb, joy savors free,
As the world bumbles, I just BE.

Solitude's Sweet Song

In the quiet of night, I dance alone,
My partner, a chair, has made it its own.
They say it's a thrill; I'm just taking a chance,
With my cat as the judge, in this one-cat dance.

The fridge hums a tune, my snack is the prize,
As I contemplate life with graham cracker sighs.
A solo duet with the snacks that I munch,
Only I can select what we have for lunch.

My sock puppet choir sings sweet lullabies,
As I giggle at shadows that dance and arise.
The moon is my audience, bright as it glows,
Each laugh is a ripple in the solitude's throes.

So here's to the nights when I'm all by myself,
With my silly routines and my thoughts on the shelf.
In this blissful embrace, I find joy out of view,
You may call it alone, but I call it a crew.

The Calm Before Dawn

The world holds its breath, wrapped in a haze,
As I wear my pajamas, a sight that betrays.
The kettle's a gurgler with coffee so strong,
It wakes the whole house with a giddy gong.

My hair's a wild tumble of night's careless art,
And the toast is burnt, yet it's made with my heart.
The birds start to chirp, they're my morning band,
While I wave to the neighbors, my breakfast in hand.

The sunshine creeps in, with a playful wink,
I'll tell it my secrets over coffee to drink.
The day's just a blank canvas, the world's my own stage,
Where laughter and chaos take center in rage.

The calm holds a promise of mischief to come,
As I juggle my tasks like a gleeful clown's drum.
With a giggle I greet the day's jumbled beat,
In the calm before dawn, life feels oh-so sweet.

Beneath Velvet Skies

Under velvet skies, I gaze up in awe,
At the wiggling stars, they've got cosmic flaws.
A comet zooms by; is it lost on its way?
I would join it, but first, I need a quick lay.

The moon beams a smile, like a pie in the night,
And I chuckle at clouds that float like a kite.
The wind's got a tickle, dancing through the trees,
Whispering secrets on a chorus of breeze.

Each twinkle above looks like it's auditioning,
For a role in my dreams, with cosmic conditioning.
The night's a big party, an offbeat ballet,
Where laughter's the music that carries away.

So here's to the wonders that float in the air,
Like my neighbor's lost cat, who really doesn't care.
Beneath velvet skies, with a grin and a sigh,
With chaos and chuckles, we reach for the high.

The Embrace of Ebb and Flow

At the shore, where the giggles romp in the spray,
The waves give a hug, then they dance far away.
My toes in the sand, they wiggle and squeal,
As the sea gently whispers, 'Let's make this a deal.'

The gulls swoop like jesters, they cackle and call,
As a beach ball bounces and starts its own brawl.
I duck from the splash, then I launch a beach snack,
In a sandy rebellion, I'm not holding back!

Shells tumble like jokesters, each with a new tale,
With an oceanic grin, they sail without fail.
The tide takes a bow, just to rise up and play,
In this dance of madness, we're here for the day.

So here's to the moments when chaos finds time,
In the embrace of the waves, there's a rhythm and rhyme.

With each ebbing giggle and flowing delight,
We find joy in the madness that colors our night.

www.ingramcontent.com/pod-product-compliance
Lightning Source LLC
Chambersburg PA
CBHW072122070526
44585CB00016B/1526